The War of the Worlds

H. G. Wells

Abridged and adapted by Janice Greene

Illustrated by Carol Stutz

A PACEMAKER CLASSIC

Fearon/Janus/Quercus
Belmont, California

Simon & Schuster Education Group

Pacemaker Classics

The Adventures of Huckleberry Finn
The Adventures of Tom Sawyer
The Call of the Wild
A Christmas Carol
Crime and Punishment
David Copperfield
The Deerslayer
Dr. Jekyll and Mr. Hyde
Ethan Frome
Frankenstein
Great Expectations
Heart of Darkness
The Hunchback of Notre Dame
Jane Eyre
The Jungle Book
The Last of the Mohicans

The Mayor of Casterbridge
Moby Dick
The Moonstone
O Pioneers!
The Prince and the Pauper
The Red Badge of Courage
Robinson Crusoe
The Scarlet Letter
A Tale of Two Cities
The Three Musketeers
The Time Machine
Treasure Island
20,000 Leagues Under the Sea
Two Years Before the Mast
The War of the Worlds
Wuthering Heights

Library of Congress Catalog Card Number: 92–72584

ISBN 0–8224–9345–4

Printed in the United States of America

2. 10 9 8
MA

Contents

1 The Coming of the Martians

No one would have believed that in the last years of the 19th century, all of our world was being watched. We had all been going about our business day by day, very sure of ourselves. We did not think much about other planets. We surely never dreamed that they might be dangerous to us. We cared only that we ruled Earth.

Some men did think there might be other men on Mars. But they assumed these men were probably not as smart as we. However, the minds of the Martians were far, far greater than ours. From the depths of outer space, the Martians were watching our planet as one might watch tiny things under a microscope. They watched, and they decided they wanted our planet. Slowly, they drew up their plans against us.

We knew that Mars was much older than Earth. It was dying, and as it died, it grew colder. The Martians knew they couldn't live there much longer. Their only hope was to find a warmer planet.

They needed our Earth. They regarded all of us who lived here almost as we regarded monkeys. Yet were they any less kind than man has been? We must remember what man has done to the buffalo and the dodo as well as to such races as the Tasmanians. We have cruelly wiped them out.

It was six years ago that the Martians came. Mars had moved opposite Earth, and then one night, a great flame of gas shot out from Mars. It headed toward Earth.

I first heard the news from Ogilvy, the well-known astronomer. He had been watching Mars since the night before and had seen the flame of gas. The next night he invited me to join him at his telescope.

The two of us watched until one o'clock in the morning. As I was taking a turn at the telescope, I saw another great flame shoot away from Mars.

A few nights later, I took a walk with my wife. We looked up at the stars, and I pointed out Mars to her. On the way home, we saw the bright red, green, and yellow signal lights of a train flashing against the sky. It was a warm night, safe and peaceful.

Then came the first falling star. Ogilvy thought the meteorite had fallen nearby, so he went looking for it soon after dawn. Near Horsell Common he found what had fallen. The thing had made a huge pit in the earth when it landed. Ogilvy went closer and looked inside the pit. What he saw did not look like a meteorite. It was a sort of metal cylinder, almost buried in the sand. The thing was so hot from its long fall that he could not get close to it.

Then he heard a noise. The top of the cylinder was moving!

"Good heavens!" Ogilvy said to himself. "There's a man—or men—in it. Burning up from the heat! Trying to get out!" All at once he knew what the great flame of gas on Mars had been: the firing of this cylinder.

He ran off wildly toward town. He came upon a stranger and tried to tell him the story of the thing he had just seen. But the man thought Ogilvy was crazy. He tried, without success, to shut Ogilvy up in a room in a public building.

Ogilvy was more careful after that. Walking along

farther, he saw Henderson in his garden. Henderson was a newspaper writer for the London paper. Ogilvy told him everything.

Ogilvy called, "Henderson! You saw that shooting star last night?"

"Well?" said Henderson.

"It's out on Horsell Common now," said Ogilvy.

"Good Lord!" said Henderson. "Fallen meteorite! That's good."

"But it's something more than a meteorite. It's a cylinder. A cylinder that something—someone—has made! And there's something inside."

Henderson stood up with his spade in his hand. "What's that?" he said. He was deaf in one ear.

Ogilvy told him everything. Henderson thought it over for a minute. Then he dropped his spade, grabbed his jacket, and joined Ogilvy in the road.

The two men hurried back to Horsell Common. By then the cylinder had stopped moving. They thought the men inside must be dead. Ogilvy and Henderson went back to town to get help. Henderson stopped at the train station and sent a telegram to his newspaper in London.

Soon a number of men and boys started out for Horsell Common. They wanted to see "the dead men from Mars." I first heard about the cylinder from a newspaper boy. I lost no time in going out toward the common.

When I arrived, there were 20 or so people already at Horsell Common. Four or five boys were sitting at the edge of the pit. They were having a good time throwing rocks at the cylinder until I stopped them. There were people on bicycles, a girl with a baby, and a gardener who had worked for me. Gregg the butcher was there with his little boy.

When I got close to the cylinder, I saw how strange it was. It seemed to be made of metal, but I had never seen a metal like this. I was sure the thing had come from Mars. Still, I did not believe there was anything alive inside.

I stayed for several hours, and the cylinder did not move or change. Then I went home and tried to work at my desk, but I could not keep my mind on my writing.

When I went back to Horsell Common, the crowd had grown. There were many carts and bicycles standing about. Many people from nearby towns must have walked there, though the day was very hot. A boy was selling green apples and ginger beer.

I went up to the edge of the pit and saw Henderson, Ogilvy, and a tall man named Stent inside. I learned later that Stent was the royal astronomer. With them were several workmen. The workmen were clearing off sand from the cylinder with spades and picks.

I went home again to have tea. When I returned to

the pit once more, it was almost dark. As I drew closer, I heard Stent's voice warning everyone, "Keep back! Keep back!"

Stent, Ogilvy, and Henderson were no longer in the pit but standing at its edge.

A boy came running toward me. "It's moving!" he said. "It's unscrewing and unscrewing! I don't like it. I'm going home, I am."

There must have been two or three hundred people around the pit then. They were shoving and pushing to see the cylinder. Even one or two ladies were there. They were pushing as much as the men and the boys were.

Someone yelled, "He's fallen in the pit!"

Just then I saw a young man in the pit. The crowd had accidentally pushed him in.

"Keep back!" others shouted.

The crowd moved back a little. Everyone seemed very excited. I heard a strange humming sound coming from the pit.

Then Ogilvy called out to someone, "I say! Help keep these idiots back! We don't know what's inside the thing, you know!"

The lid of the cylinder was moving again. Then it came off. It fell to the ground with a loud ringing sound. I looked inside. All I could see was blackness. Then I saw two shining eyes. A tentacle, like a gray snake, came wiggling out and up into the air. Then another tentacle reached out.

A chill came over me. A woman screamed. People began pushing back from the edge of the pit. Their faces turned from surprise to horror. Some began to run. The young man in the pit was still trying to climb over the edge of it. I watched, but I could not move.

A big gray thing was coming out of the cylinder. It was about the size of a bear. As it rose up, I could see its skin, like wet leather. Two dark eyes stared at me. It was panting, and its mouth dripped spit. It was having trouble breathing in our atmosphere. The heavy pull of earth's gravity made it hard for the thing to move, as well.

All at once, it fell. I heard a thud, like a heap of leather hitting the ground, followed by a strange, thick cry. Then another Martian appeared.

I turned and ran madly for the trees. But I ran and fell and ran in a crazy way, for I could not turn my eyes away from those things.

I stood among the trees, panting. There was a small dark shape at the edge of the pit. It was the man who had fallen in. He got his knee up, but then he seemed to slip. All at once he went out of sight. I thought I heard him scream, but I was too frightened to help him.

Most of the crowd had gathered in groups of two or three. A man came up to me. "What ugly brutes!"

he said. "Good God, what ugly brutes!" He said it over and over again.

It grew darker. Nothing in the pit seemed to move. A few people walked up to the pit, looked in, and backed away. Then Ogilvy, Stent, Henderson, and a few others walked up to the pit. They carried a white flag.

Suddenly, there was a flash of light. Three puffs of bright green smoke rose up from the pit. The men's lighted faces now looked green. A humming sound came from the cylinder while a dark shape rose slowly out of the pit. Then a thin ray of light shot out. As the light touched each man, he burst into flames.

The flashing light swung through the crowd. It was like a sword of heat. Pine trees burst into fire. Every bush became a mass of flames. Death jumped from man to man. The loud crackle of fire was everywhere. A horse squealed, then made no sound.

Then, all at once, the humming stopped. The dark shape sank back into the pit.

Everything happened so quickly that I had not moved. Had the sword of heat made a full circle, I would have been dead, too. Suddenly Horsell Common seemed completely empty of men. The houses toward the train station sent up towers of flame into the night air. All the rest was dark. I felt terribly alone. I turned and ran. I cried without a sound, as a child might do.

2 The Fighting Begins

We still don't know how the Martians are able to kill men so quickly and quietly. The best guess suggests that the Martians produce the intense heat in a special chamber. Then they project the heat against their targets with the use of a polished mirror. We use a similar type of mirror here on Earth to project light from lighthouses. We do know that the Martians' terrible heat rays can make lead run like water. They can soften iron, melt glass, and make water explode into steam.

But I knew nothing that night. I only felt fear. I ran until I was worn out. Then I fell and lay still. I must have been there for some time. When I finally got up, my mind was a blank wonder.

A train went by, flying south. A group of people stood by the gate of a nearby house, talking. It was all so real. But to think of what lay behind me in Horsell Common! The things I saw could not have happened!

I stopped a group of people. "What news from the common?" I said. "Have you heard of the men from Mars? The creatures from Mars?"

"Yes, quite enough, thanks," said the woman

over the gate. Then they all laughed.

I staggered home and met my wife at the door. She was shocked at how worn and worried I looked. I went into the dining room, sat down, and drank some wine. After a while, I was able to tell her what I had seen.

She believed all that I told her; she was frightened.

"There is one thing," I said. "They are very sluggish. They may kill people who come near the pit, but they cannot get out of it. . . . Oh, the horror of them!"

"Don't, dear!" said my wife. She put her hand on mine.

"Poor Oglivy!" I said. "To think that he may be lying there dead!" Then I saw that my wife's face was deadly white. I stopped talking.

Soon the food and wine made me feel braver, and I tried to comfort my wife. "The Martians have done a foolish thing," I said. "But we probably scared them quite a lot. Perhaps they did not expect to find living beings here. I am sure they did not expect to find beings as smart as we."

I added, "We can always fire a shell into the pit. If worst comes to worst, we will kill them all."

I remember that dinner so well. I remember my wife's sweet, worried face. I can see now the white tablecloth and the silver and the glasses. I didn't

know it, but that was the last good meal I would have for many strange and terrible days. The news of the Martians spread slowly. Outside our small district, no one knew what had happened at Horsell Common.

In London, they thought poor Henderson's telegram was a joke. The newspaper sent a wire to check his story, but he didn't reply—for he was dead. His story was never printed.

Most of the district went about its business the same as always. People ate their dinners. Men dug in their gardens after a day's work. Children were put to bed. Young people walked through the lanes, in love. Students sat over their books. People rattling home on the London train might have seen a red glow from Horsell Common. But they would have thought that it was only a brush fire.

Around the common, though, a crowd remained. It was mostly silent except for the sound of Martians moving about and hammering. Every now and then, a puff of greenish white smoke rose up into the starry sky.

At eleven that night, a group of soldiers arrived at the common. They formed a ring around it. The military understood this was serious business.

Just before midnight, the crowd saw a star fall from the sky. It flashed bright green, then went down in the pine woods to the northeast.

A second cylinder had fallen to Earth.

The next day, I walked outside before breakfast and saw my neighbor in his garden. He said, "It's a pity the Martians won't let us close to them. I'd like to know how they live on another planet. We might learn a thing or two."

He came up to the fence and gave me a handful of strawberries. He always shared fresh food from his garden. Then we talked about "poor Ogilvy."

After breakfast, instead of working, I walked toward the common. With so many soldiers gathered there, the Martians seemed quite helpless in their pit. It hardly seemed a fair fight.

That afternoon, I heard the thud of guns coming from the north. The second cylinder was being shelled. They wanted to kill the Martians inside before it opened.

Our neighborhood was quiet until six o'clock. I was sitting at tea with my wife when suddenly the firing began. Then there was a huge crash close by that shook the ground. I ran out on the lawn. The tops of the trees burst into flame. The tower of a little church nearby broke off and slid away. One of our chimneys cracked. A piece flew off and landed in the flower bed. Then, for a moment, it was quiet.

I gripped my wife's arm and ran her out to the road. Then I brought out our servant. "We can't stay here," I said, as the firing began again.

"But where are we to go?" asked my wife, in terror. I remembered her cousin in Leatherhead. "Leatherhead!" I shouted above the noise.

She looked away from me, down the hill. People were coming out of their houses, amazed.

"How are we to get to Leatherhead?" she said.

"Wait here," I said. "You are safe here." I started off at once to the Spotted Dog, a restaurant nearby. I knew the landlord had a horse and cart.

I found him talking to another man. He was saying, "I want a pound for it. And I don't have a driver."

"I'll give you two pounds," I said, over the other man's shoulder.

"What do you want it for?"

"And I'll bring it back by midnight," I said. With that he gave me the cart.

I put a few of our best things, including our silver, into a tablecloth. As I was coming out of the house, a soldier came running by. He was telling people to leave their houses. I loaded our things into the cart, then rode away down Maybury Hill. I picked up my wife at once.

The road in front of us was quiet and sunny. Up ahead, I saw our doctor's cart racing along. I turned my head to see the hill we were leaving. Fire and smoke were driving up into the still air. The road was dotted with people running in our direction.

I could hear the whirr of a machine gun and the crack of rifles.

I hit the horse hard with the whip. We passed the doctor's cart after the next town.

Soon after we had left Maybury Hill, the firing stopped. The rest of the trip was quiet. The roadside was sweet with roses, and the smell of hay was in the air. We got to Leatherhead about nine o'clock. The horse had an hour's rest while I had supper.

My wife had been strangely quiet on the trip. I think she wanted me to stay in Leatherhead that night. How I wish I had! Still, I had promised to return the cart to Maybury Hill. I remember how white my wife's face was as we said goodbye.

For my part, I was quite excited. I was not very sorry I had to go back to Maybury Hill that night. I think what I really wanted was to be there when the Martians were killed.

3   In the Storm

The night was very dark, hot, and close. As I came through the town of Ockham, I saw a blood-red glow from the hills far ahead. Red and black smoke mixed with the clouds of a coming storm.

All at once through the clouds came a thread of green fire. It was a third cylinder falling to Earth!

Right behind it danced the first lightning of the storm. Thunder burst like a rocket over my head. The horse took the bit between his teeth and ran.

We flew down a slope toward the foot of Maybury Hill. Flash after flash of lightning filled the sky. Claps of thunder mixed with a strange crackling noise. A thin hail hit my face as I drove.

All at once I saw something moving on Maybury Hill. I peered through the flashes of lightning. Then in one great flash I saw it! A huge tripod—higher than many houses, a monster of shining metal— covered a hundred yards in a single step. It crashed through the pine trees, smashing them apart as it came.

Then a second fighting machine appeared. It seemed to be rushing right toward me. At the sight of the second monster, I lost my nerve. I pulled the horse's head hard to the right. The cart tumbled over onto the horse. I flew out and fell into a puddle of water.

I crawled out and hid behind some bushes. The horse lay still (his neck was broken, poor thing!). In another moment, the huge fighting machine walked by me.

Up close, there was something alive about the fighting machine. A hood at the top of it moved back and forth. It seemed like a head looking about. As it passed, it gave off a loud terrible noise: "Aloo! Aloo!" Then it joined the first machine, which was bending over something in the field. I am sure they were looking at the third cylinder.

I found a ditch nearby. I crawled along it until I reached the woods near Maybury Hill.

The rain was falling very hard as I climbed up the hill. I held on to the fence and worked my way along in the blackness. Water from the storm swept down the road.

Near the top I tripped over something soft. Lightning flashed, and I could see a heap of black cloth and a pair of boots. I waited for another flash. It came, and I saw this was the body of a man lying there. It looked as if the man had been thrown against the fence. This was the landlord of the Spotted Dog.

I stepped over the body carefully and made my

way up the street to my house. Toward Maybury Bridge, I heard voices and the sound of feet. But I did not have the nerve to shout or to go to them. I unlocked the door and let myself in. I walked to the foot of the stairs and sat down. My mind was full of those walking metal giants and the body that was smashed against the fence.

After a while, I noticed little pools of water about me on the rug. I hadn't noticed how wet I was. I drank some whisky and went to change my clothes.

I looked out the window. The storm was over. The common was glowing bright red. Across the light, huge black shapes moved back and forth. It seemed as if the whole country in that direction was on fire. Tongues of flame burned everywhere, turning the clouds bright red. I looked out toward the train station. Many of the nearby houses were wrecks, still glowing with fire. The train was wrecked. Half of its cars were smashed and burning.

Except for what was lit by fire, all around me was blackness. And this was the little world where I had been living for years! What had happened in the last few hours I did not know.

I watched the great black machines moving about the common. Could these fighting machines think for themselves? I felt that was impossible. Or did a Martian sit inside, the way a man's brain sits inside his body? I began to compare the fighting machines

18

with the machines of humans. The Martian machines made ours seem terribly simple.

The sky cleared. Mars was just dropping into the west when a soldier came into my garden.

I leaned out the window. "Hist!" I said in a whisper.

The man stepped softly across the lawn. "Who's there?" he whispered.

"Where are you going?" I asked.

"God knows," he said.

"Are you trying to hide?"

"That's it."

"Come into the house," I said. I brought him inside.

"My God!" he said, as I let him in.

"What has happened?" I asked.

"What hasn't?" he made a wild gesture. "They wiped us out—just wiped us out."

I sat him down and gave him some whisky. He finished it, then put his head down on the table and sobbed like a little boy. It was a long time before he could talk. He told me he was a driver in the artillery. The gun he drove was stationed near Horsell Common.

At first, there was firing in the common, and the Martians were crawling to their second cylinder. They used a metal shield to protect themselves.

Once our guns were brought out, the fighting started. The artilleryman was riding to the rear when his horse tripped over a rabbit hole. He was

thrown into a ditch. At that moment the gun behind him was blown up. Fire was everywhere. He found himself lying under a heap of dead men and horses.

He said, "A minute before, it was just like we were on parade. Then—bang, swish! Wiped out!"

The artilleryman had stayed hidden in the ditch

for a long time. A fighting machine began to walk around the common. The Martian inside swept the ground with a heat ray. In a few minutes, every living thing, every bush and tree, was dead.

Then the machine walked to the train station. Again the heat ray did its work. It wrecked the train. Then it turned, and the houses at Woking Station were turned into burning heaps. In one night, the valley had become a valley of ashes.

Finally, the fighting machine walked away toward the second cylinder. When a second machine walked away with the first, the artilleryman was able to make his escape.

4 More Destruction

At dawn, the artilleryman and I left Maybury Hill. The artilleryman wanted to report to the general at Weybridge. I was headed toward Leatherhead—and my wife. A cylinder was between my house and Leatherhead, but I thought I would risk it. The artilleryman talked me into taking the long way around. After all, I did not want to make my wife a widow.

I wanted to start out right away, but again, the artilleryman knew better. He made me find a flask for whisky. Then we filled our pockets with biscuits and meat.

We made our way down the road, past charred bodies, broken furniture, and small valuables that people had dropped. After a while, we left the burned houses and trees behind.

The town of Byfleet had not been touched by the heat ray. There, soldiers were going from house to house, telling people to pack up and leave. But people would not believe they were in danger.

We saw one old fellow with a huge box. It was filled with orchids and flower pots. He was arguing with a soldier who said he should leave it behind.

I said to the old man, "Do you know what's over there?" I pointed at the pine trees that hid the Martians.

"Eh?" said the old man. "I was trying to tell the man these flowers are valuable."

"Death!" I shouted. "Death is coming! Death!" I ran to catch up with the artilleryman. When I looked back, the old man was standing by his box, staring at the trees.

Soon we arrived at Weybridge. There, a large, noisy crowd was waiting to cross the river. There were many more people than there were boats to carry them. People were arriving every minute, panting along with heavy loads. One husband and wife were even carrying a small door. It was piled high with things they had taken from their house.

Some soldiers stood laughing at the crowd. Others were gathered at attention in a long line. People seemed to think the Martians were just strong human beings. They thought the Martians would attack and rob the town and then be defeated.

"It's bows and arrows against the lightning," said the artilleryman. "They haven't seen the heat ray yet."

Then we heard a thud—the sound of a gun. Hidden soldiers had fired from the trees across the river. A woman screamed. The crowd stood still beside the river. We could not see what the soldiers were firing at.

A woman beside me said, "The soldiers will stop 'em." But she did not sound so sure.

Suddenly, the ground moved under our feet, and the air seemed to shake. Two or three windows smashed in the houses nearby.

"Here they are!" shouted a man in the crowd. "Yonder! Do you see them? Yonder!"

Quickly, one after another—one, two, three, four —the fighting machines appeared. They were far away, across the flat ground. But they came toward the river as fast as flying birds. Then, from another direction, came a fifth fighting machine.

The fifth machine swept swiftly toward the guns. Its metal body shone brightly in the sun. It held a heat ray high in the air.

"Get underwater!" I shouted. I threw myself into the river. Others did the same.

In two steps, the machine walked through the water to the other side of the river. It was raising up the heat ray when a shot was fired from the trees.

Two more shots rang out. The hood of the fighting machine twisted about. Then a fourth shell hit it in the face. The Martian inside was killed.

"Hit!" I shouted.

The machine kept moving, like a drunken giant. It hit the tower of a church, then turned aside and fell

into the river upstream. As it crashed, water, mud, and pieces of metal flew into the air. The heat ray hit the river, and a huge wave of nearly boiling water rushed downstream. Steam filled the air. I heard the screams of people in the distance as the hot water reached them.

Thick clouds of steam rose from the wrecked machine. It waved its arms and legs like a dying animal, and brown fluid spurted up out of it.

Then the other fighting machines arrived. Two of them bent over the destroyed machine and its dead Martian. The other machines aimed their heat rays and fired. Houses crashed to the ground. Trees and fences flashed into flame. The heat ray swept across the river. People were hopping out of the river just as little frogs hop through the grass to escape man.

In a moment, a huge, hot wave was on me. I screamed. I hurried through the hissing water, burning my hands. Finally, I staggered out onto the beach and fell down on the gravel—right in the way of a Martian. I expected nothing but death.

But the machine—and the Martian inside—walked past me. The four machines gathered around the dead Martian. They lifted up the dead Martian within its destroyed machine and carried it away.

If they had left their dead friend behind and pushed on, the Martians would have reached London easily. But they were in no hurry. Every night, a new cylinder fell, bringing more Martians.

On our side, the military worked madly. Every minute a fresh gun was made ready. Before night fell, many a row of houses on the way to London were hiding guns.

While the Martians were getting ready for the next battle, I headed in the direction of London.

I found a small boat. For a long time I drifted down the river. The sun blazed down on me. I tried to paddle as much as my burned hands would let me. Finally, I landed the boat and lay down in the grass. I felt very sick.

I must have fallen asleep. When I opened my eyes, a man was sitting near me.

"Have you any water?" I asked.

"You have been asking for water for the last half hour," he said. He was a clergyman, with a weak face and pale blue eyes. He stared off into the distance.

"What does it mean?" he asked. "Why are these terrible Martians here? What wrong have we done?"

"Are we far from the town of Sunbury?" I asked.

"What are we to do?" he asked. "Has Earth been given over to these Martians?"

"Are we far from Sunbury?" I repeated.

"All the work . . . all the Sunday schools . . . what have we done? What has Weybridge done? The church! We rebuilt it three years ago! Gone!" he said.

"Things have changed," I said, quietly. "You must

keep your head. There is still hope."

"Hope!" he said. "This is the beginning of the end!"

I laid my hand on his shoulder. "Be a man!" I said. "What good is religion if it cannot stand up now? Think of what floods and wars have done to men! Did you think God had exempted Weybridge? He is not an insurance agent."

"But how can we escape? They have no weakness and no pity."

"That cannot be true," I said. "One of them was killed less than three hours ago. And the stronger they are, the smarter we must be."

"Killed!" he said. "How can a punishment from God be killed?"

"I saw it happen," I told him. I added, "The Martians will be coming this way again. Come, we had better follow this path—to the north."

5 In London

At the time the Martians came, my younger brother lived in London. He was studying to be a doctor.

My brother first heard about the Martians from the Saturday newspaper. It carried a short article about what had happened in Horsell Common. It said the Martians had been frightened by the crowd. They had killed a number of people with a quick-firing gun. But the story said the Martians could not get out of the pit where they had landed.

My brother did not worry about us. He knew our house was a good two miles away from Horsell Common.

The next day brought a different story. It said the Martians had come out of the pit, under armor, and destroyed Woking Station.

Still, London remained calm. Most people there do not read the Sunday paper. Besides, they had the habit of thinking London could not be hurt.

My brother read the paper that Sunday, however. He quickly made his way down to the station and found that all of the trains had been delayed. Everyone at the station seemed cranky.

One man told him, "There are all sorts of people coming in from Weybridge. Soldiers told them to leave because the Martians were coming. What the dickens does it all mean? The Martians can't get out of their pit, can they?"

My brother could not tell him.

That evening, my brother saw men running out into the street with fresh newspapers to sell. The ink on the papers was still wet. The men shouted, "Fighting in Weybridge! The Martians retreat! London in danger!"

When my brother read that evening's paper, he understood the full power of the Martians. They were far from helpless. Their minds were so great that they used machines to act as their bodies. Our biggest guns could not stand against them.

The story in the paper reported that the Martians' fighting machines looked like huge spiders, one hundred feet high. They could move as fast as an express train and shoot out a ray of great heat. Five of the Martians had been moving toward the Thames in these machines. One, by happy chance, had been killed. The other Martians had killed a number of soldiers with the heat ray. After that, they had gone back to their cylinders.

Meanwhile, the story went on, the military was bringing guns from all over the country. Most of the guns were put in place to cover London. If any more cylinders fell, the military would try to blow them up.

The story ended with a request that people not panic. True, the Martians were dangerous. But there were probably no more than twenty of them. And England had millions of people.

My brother walked toward Trafalgar Square. He saw refugees who had come from the direction of the fighting. He saw a man and his wife and two boys pulling a cartload of furniture. Close behind was a hay wagon full of five or six people with boxes. They all looked worn out and dirty.

My brother feared the worst for me. He read and reread the paper. He went home and tried to study but could not. About midnight he went to bed. But a few hours later he was awakened. From outside came the sound of door knockers, running feet, ringing bells, and distant drums. Red light danced on the ceiling.

My brother stuck his head out of the window. A policeman was hammering on the doors. "The Martians are coming!" he shouted.

Then came the shouts of men selling newspapers: "Hundreds killed in the Thames Valley!"

All around the great city of London, people were waking up and rubbing their sore eyes. They were opening up their windows to stare outside and ask questions. Last night everyone had gone to bed

peacefully. Now they were waking up to fear.

My brother went outside. Every moment there were more people on the street.

"Black smoke!" he heard people saying. "Black smoke!"

He bought another paper, which cost him a whole shilling. The paper carried a message from the commander in chief. He reported that the Martians' fighting machines were able to shoot out huge clouds of black, poisonous smoke by means of rockets. The Martians had destroyed Richmond, Kingston, and Wimbledon. They were coming toward London. They were destroying everything on the way. It was impossible to stop them.

That was all, but it was enough. The six million people of London were stirring, moving, running. Soon they would be pouring out of the city.

"Black smoke!" the voices cried. My brother ran back to his room, put all his money—ten shillings— in his pocket, and went out again into the streets.

6 Defeat

While I was listening to the clergyman's wild talk in Weybridge, my brother was watching people pour out of London. At the same time, the Martians were attacking the Thames Valley.

Three Martians had used their heat ray on several batteries near Ripley. Few men had escaped. About nine that night, those three Martians were joined by four others in their fighting machines.

The new Martian fighting machines carried thick black tubes. They also gave tubes to the other three. The seven of them stood in a long curved line between St. George's Hill, Weybridge, and the village of Send.

Then four more Martians arrived. The clergyman and I were walking on the road from Halliford when two of them passed close by. We hid in a ditch and watched. One of them stopped and stood facing Sunbury. The other stood in the distance, near Staines. These also carried black tubes.

All eleven Martian machines now stood in a great half circle. They formed a line about twelve miles long. Standing in their still and tall fighting machines, the Martians seemed to own the night.

The clergyman cried out in fear and began to run, but I knew that running from a Martian would do no good. I crawled into a ditch by the side of the road. When the clergyman looked back and saw me, he decided to join me there.

Behind houses and trees and bushes, all over the Thames Valley, guns were waiting. As soon as the Martians came close, the firing would begin.

Did the Martians know how well trained—how ready—we were? Or did they think of us as stinging bees in a hive? Did they think they could destroy us all? (At the time, no one knew what kind of food they needed.)

After what seemed like a terribly long wait, I heard a sound like the shot of a gun. Then came another and another. And then the Martian near us raised up its tube and fired a shot. There was no flash, no smoke, just the sound of firing.

I was so excited that I forgot the danger and my burned hands. I climbed up out of the ditch and stared toward Sunbury. I expected to see smoke or fire. But all I saw was the deep blue sky above and a single star. Below was the mist of evening.

"What has happened?" said the clergyman.

"Heaven knows!" I said. Every moment I expected the guns below to fire back. But the evening was silent.

We climbed higher. Toward Sunbury, something dark, like a black cloud, was rising from the ground.

Far away, we heard the Martians hooting to one another. Then the earth shook with the thud of their guns. But the soldiers below did not shoot back.

At the time, we could not understand these things. But now we know the meaning of those dark clouds. Each of the Martians had fired off a large pellet from its tube. On falling to the ground, the canisters smashed. Out of each poured an inky cloud of gas. The touch of a cloud was death.

Usually, after having done its work, the black smoke settled, leaving a thick powder over everything. The powder itself was harmless. The

Martians cleared it away with jets of steam. Thus, they got rid of us just as we might smoke out a wasp's nest.

Later that night, a fourth pellet fell. Then the great line of fighting machines went forward. They walked all that night, toward London. The soldiers never had the ghost of a chance against them. Wherever the trees might have hidden guns, the Martians fired the black smoke. If a gun chanced to fire upon them, they used the heat ray.

By midnight the burning trees lit up a huge cloud of black smoke. It covered the whole Thames Valley as far as the eye could see.

After that, no group of men would stand against the Martians. Even the crews of the torpedo boats and destroyers that had come up the Thames refused to fight.

You can guess what it must have been like in that valley as the pellets smashed open. Curls of inky clouds spread over the land. Men were running and screaming, leaving their guns behind. They would cry out, then fall rolling and choking. And then death came to all of them. Only a silent cloud remained, hiding those it had killed.

7   Panic in London

A great wave of fear swept through London. When they learned the Martians were on their way, people rushed to leave the city. By midnight trains were filling up. People fought savagely for standing room in the cars.

Near Liverpool Street Station, people were being trampled and crushed. Guns were fired. People were stabbed. Instead of protecting people, the police were breaking heads. As the day wore on, the crowds grew even greater. My brother tried to get on a train at Chalk Farm, but he could not get through the crowd.

On Chalk Farm Road, people had broken into a bicycle shop. My brother had the luck to get a bicycle, which he rode to Edgeware. There he thought about what to do next. He thought he might go northeast, to Chelmsford, where some friends lived.

He took a grass path eastward toward High Barnet. On this path he met the two ladies with whom he ended up traveling. He had come just in time to save them.

He had heard their screams and hurried around a

corner. There he saw two men trying to drag the women out of their pony cart. A third man held the frightened pony's head. One of the ladies, a short woman dressed in white, was simply screaming. The other, a dark, slender woman, was using her whip on the man who held the pony's head.

My brother shouted and ran up to them. One of the men turned to hit him. My brother, who is a very good boxer, knocked him against the wheel of the cart. It was no time for fairness, so he laid the man out with a kick.

He grabbed the collar of the man who pulled at the slender lady. Then a third man hit him between the eyes.

Suddenly, the cart took off down the lane with the women in it. My brother ran after them, but he tripped and fell. When he got up, two of the men had caught up with him. He would have been out of luck had the slender lady not turned back to help him. She had a gun with her. It had been under the seat of the cart.

The slender lady fired, almost hitting my brother. One of the robbers took off. The other followed, swearing at the first for being a coward. The third man was still knocked out.

The slender lady turned to my brother. "Take this!" she said, and gave him the gun. They returned together to the cart.

"I'll sit here if I may," said my brother. He got up on the empty front seat.

"Give me the reins," said the slender lady. She laid the whip on the pony's side. In another moment, the robbers were out of sight.

Thus my brother found himself with a cut lip, traveling on a strange road with two strange women.

He learned that his companions were a Miss and a Mrs. Elphinstone, the younger sister and the wife of a doctor in Stanmore. The doctor had learned about the Martians and put the women in the cart to escape. He had stayed behind to tell the neighbors about the Martians, planning to catch up with the women in Edgeware. There they were going to get on a train. But Edgeware was jammed with traffic, so the women had turned into this side road. My brother promised to stay with them, but he felt it was unsafe to stay where they were. After describing what he had seen so far, he urged them to flee.

The slender woman—Miss Elphinstone—thought they might drive to another train station. But my brother said they should drive to the coast. From there, they could find a boat and leave the country.

So off they went. The first step was to cross the Great North Road. As they drew closer, they saw more and more people. Soon they heard the sounds of voices, horses' hooves, and creaking wagons.

"Good heavens!" cried Mrs. Elphinstone. "What are you driving us into?"

The road was a steady stream of people, all rushing to the north. Great clouds of white dust were thrown up by the feet of horses and men and women and by the wheels of every kind of vehicle.

The crowd was held in by the houses on both sides of the road. Everyone hurried and pushed. "Way!" they shouted. "Make way!" People on foot were driven into ditches by racing carts and horses.

"Push on!" was the cry. "Push on! The Martians are coming!"

Sad, worn-out women walked by. Many were well dressed. Their children, covered with dust, walked beside them. Their tired faces were wet with tears. With many of the women and children were men, some helpful, some savage. Fleeing side by side with them were shopkeepers, clerks, workers, and street people. There was even one poor fellow in a nightshirt with a coat thrown over it.

"Go on!" people shouted. "Go on, they are coming!"

Then my brother saw an odd-faced man with a small handbag. As he watched, the man's bag split open. A heap of gold coins fell out. They rolled here and there among the feet of men and horses. The man stopped and stared stupidly at his gold.

"Way!" cried the men all about him. "Make way!"

The man threw himself on the coins. He was shoving handfuls into his pocket. A horse and a cart were about to run him down.

"Stop!" my brother screamed at the driver of the cart. He pushed a woman out of the way and tried to grab the horse's bit. Before he could get to it, he heard a scream. A wheel of the cart passed over the poor man's back. Then the driver hit my brother across the face with his whip.

My brother yelled to the next driver, "Get him out of the road!" They grabbed the fallen man by the collar. The man fought them off, fearing for his gold.

As they struggled with the man, a carriage smashed into the stopped cart. A horse's hoof almost hit my brother's foot. He jumped back, and the fallen man disappeared beneath the wheels.

"Let us go back," shouted my brother. "We cannot cross this hell." He turned the pony around.

The women sat silent and shivering. Miss Elphinstone was very white. Her sister-in-law was weeping. My brother was confused and horrified. But after a moment, he realized there was no other way; the road had to be crossed.

My brother turned the pony around again. They forced their way into the road. My brother grabbed the reins of a cab horse and made it stop. Then Miss Elphinstone drove the pony onto the road. The angry cabman hit my brother with his whip.

My brother took the reins from Miss Elphinstone and gave her the gun. "Point it at the man behind if he begins to push us," he said. "No, point it at his horse!"

They were fiercely swept along with the crowd. They had gone several miles before they were able to work their way across that terrible road.

That night they spent sitting in the cart. They were tired, cold, and hungry, but none of them dared to sleep.

8 The *Thunder Child*

While my brother was making his escape, every other road out of London also was flooded with people. If the Martians had wanted to destroy us, they could have killed every person in London that Monday. The entire population was running through the streets. The mass of people was greater than the biggest army ever seen. Six million refugees were there—without arms or food. Many had no idea of where they were headed.

The Martians—in their fighting machines— moved slowly toward London, spreading the black smoke like a blot of ink. They did not try to destroy every human being in their way. Rather, they aimed at destroying our will to fight. They blew up powder stores, cut telegraph wires, wrecked trains.

As they made their way toward the coast, my brother and the women heard that the Martians had taken over London. That same night, a sixth cylinder had fallen at Wimbledon. (I will soon tell the story of how the fifth cylinder fell.)

My brother and the women passed that night in a field of wheat. He and Miss Elphinstone took turns keeping watch. While Miss Elphinstone was

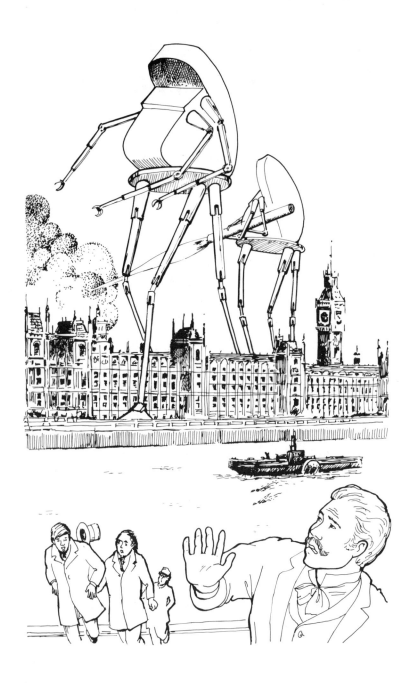

watching, the seventh cylinder fell to Earth.

The next day a group called the Committee of Public Supply seized their pony. In return, they promised them nothing but food the next day. My brother decided not to wait. Instead, the three pushed on. That afternoon, they reached Tillingham. Finally, they came within sight of the sea.

All kinds of boats were gathered there to take people out of the country. A couple of miles out was an ironclad warship, the *Thunder Child*.

As they neared the shore, Mrs. Elphinstone panicked, saying she would rather die than find herself friendless in another country. Poor thing! She seemed to think that the French would be as bad as the Martians!

When they had finally made it down to the beach, my brother found some men from a paddle steamer. The boat was going to Ostend. They agreed on a price, and the three of them went on board.

There were already a number of people in the boat. But the captain took on more and more until the boat was dangerously overcrowded.

The captain might have taken on even more people if the sound of guns hadn't begun to the south. As if in answer, the *Thunder Child* fired a small flag. Then it hoisted a string of flags.

As the steamer began moving out to sea, a Martian fighting machine appeared. It was making its way up the muddy coast. The captain was terrified—and angry that he had waited so long. He swore at the top of his lungs. My brother was more amazed than frightened.

The first fighting machine headed for the shore. Another machine appeared and then another. They were all walking toward the sea. The steamer seemed to move much too slowly.

Then the steamer turned suddenly to get out of the way. My brother fell off the chair he was standing on. When he rose, he heard people cheering. The *Thunder Child* was rushing by!

The warship tore through the waves toward the fighting machines. The three machines were now deep in the water. The Martians inside seemed puzzled by the *Thunder Child*. The warship did not fire but drove straight at them, full speed.

When the ship was very close, one of the machines lowered a tube. It shot a canister of the black gas at the warship. The canister hit the side of the ship with an inky jet of gas. Still, the *Thunder Child* drove on.

The machines moved back toward the beach. One of them raised the heat ray and fired again at the *Thunder Child*. A bank of steam rose from the water. The heat ray must have cut through the warship like scissors through paper.

Then the *Thunder Child* fired. A flame shot up

through the steam at the machine. The Martian staggered and fell. A great body of water and steam shot high into the air.

The people on the small steamer shouted together. Then they shouted again. For out of the white steam rushed the *Thunder Child*. She was on fire but still alive.

The ship headed straight for the second fighting machine. When she was a hundred yards away, the machine fired the heat ray. There was a great thud and a flash as the second heat ray hit. The machine staggered at the force of the explosion. The *Thunder Child* was a burning wreck, but still she came! She ran into the Martian, and it folded up like cardboard and fell. My brother shouted. A great cloud of steam hid everything.

"Two!" yelled the captain.

The steam hung over the water for many minutes. All this time, the small steamer was paddling out to sea. When the smoke and steam had cleared, nothing could be seen of the *Thunder Child* or of the third fighting machine.

The sun sank into gray clouds. The sky grew dark, and the evening star came into sight. All at once the captain cried out and pointed. Something very large, flat, and broad rushed up out of the clouds and into the clear sky. The object swept in a great curve and vanished into the night, raining darkness on the land.

9 The Earth Under the Martians

While my brother was traveling toward the sea, the clergyman and I were hiding in a house in Halliford. We had fled there to escape the black smoke that was all around us.

All that time, I had thought about my wife. I had worried that she might be in danger or might think that I was dead. My only hope was that the Martians were moving toward London, leaving her safe in Leatherhead.

I was sick of the clergyman. All he could think about—or talk about—was his own sadness. I went to stay in a child's room. When he followed me there, I moved to a room at the top of the house and locked myself in.

The black smoke was creeping nearer all the time, moving in from every direction. After two days, a Martian came by. From inside its fighting machine it cleared away the black smoke with a jet of steam. The steam hissed against the walls of the house, smashed windows, and burned the clergyman's hand.

When we looked out of the house, the gas had gone. Everything was covered with the harmless black dust, as if a black snow had fallen. We were free to leave, but the clergyman wished to stay where we were.

"We are safe here," he said. "Safe here."

I decided to leave him there. (How I wish I had!) I thought of what the artilleryman had taught me and looked for food and drink. I found oil and rags for my burns. I found some clothes in one of the bedrooms. Seeing that I was truly going, the clergyman decided to come along after all.

All along the road lay the bodies of people and horses, thickly covered with black dust. It made me think of the last days of Pompeii.

We got to Hampton Court safely and were glad to see a small patch of green amid the blackness. We went through Bushey Park to Twickenham. Twickenham had been left unharmed!

Suddenly, we saw people running. We looked up and saw a fighting machine looming over the housetops. If the Martian inside had seen us, we would have been killed. We dashed into a nearby garden shed and hid.

I could not stop thinking about Leatherhead. Soon I left the shed and started on my way. I had left the clergyman behind, but he came running after me.

That second trip was the most foolish I had ever made. It was clear that the Martians were nearby. Within minutes we saw a Martian pursue five little black figures. They ran from its fighting machine, but the Martian picked them all up one by one. It tossed them into a metal basket hanging over the shoulder of its fighting machine.

It was the first time I had seen that the Martians wanted more than just to kill us. They wanted to keep some of us. For a moment we were unable to move. Then we fled through a gate into a walled garden. We fell into a ditch and lay there in scared silence.

It was late when we went out once again, into a sea of dead bodies and smashed carriages. My partner kept saying he was hungry and thirsty, so we went to look for food.

At last we came to a house on the way to Morlake. Inside we found two loaves of bread, half of a ham, and cans of soup and fish. We didn't know it then, but we were to live on this food for many days to come.

We ate a meal in the dark. "It must be about midnight," I said, and then came a bright flash of green light. Everything in the kitchen shone briefly in green and black, then disappeared into darkness again.

Then followed the greatest crash I had ever heard. There was a thud behind me and then the smashing of glass. Plaster from the ceiling fell on our heads. I was thrown across the floor against the oven handle. It knocked me out for some time. When I came to, the clergyman was dabbing water on my forehead.

"Are you better?" he asked in a whisper.

I sat up.

"Don't move," he said. "The floor is covered with broken dishes. You can't possibly move without making a noise, and they are out there."

I listened. From outside, very close, came a rattling sound.

We sat still until daylight, when we saw that most of the house around us had fallen. Outside, dirt was piled high, covering the broken window. There was a small hole in the wall. Through it, we could see a fighting machine moving about.

All at once I knew what had happened.

"The fifth cylinder," I whispered. "The fifth shot from Mars has hit this house!"

"God have mercy upon us!" whispered the clergyman. I could hear him crying quietly.

Soon we heard hammering, loud hooting noises, and then hissing, like the hissing of an engine. The next day, we saw a new Martian machine.

The thing was like a great metal spider. It moved on five shining legs. About its body were tentacles that could reach and grab like arms. It was working with a number of rods, plates, and bars to make the walls of the cylinder stronger. It moved so quickly

and perfectly that at first it did not seem like a machine.

In the days that followed, we were able to watch the Martians very closely. Outside of their machines they had no bodies at all, only huge round heads. Their eyes were large and dark; they seemed to have no noses. Their mouths were fleshy beaks, and around each grew sixteen tentacles.

The Martians did not eat with their mouths. Instead, they took the fresh blood of living things—humans—and injected it. Before they ate, they always made a loud hooting sound.

This way of eating may fill us with horror. But we should remember how awful our meat-eating habits must seem to an animal like a rabbit. Injecting food made sense to the Martians. It saved them the time and energy of chewing, and it helped them survive.

Later we learned much more about the Martians: We learned that they did not sleep. We learned that they had no gender. We saw a young Martian born here on earth. It budded off from its parent, just as a plant bulb might grow from a bud.

We learned, too, that Martian plants grew much as ours did. A red weed grew here for a time and showed us that red, not green, was the usual plant color on Mars.

The red weed didn't last long on Earth, but while it grew, it was lively and full. The weed spread quickly through the countryside, taking root wherever there was a stream of water.

There is one more difference between Martian life and our own, though I did not know it at the time. There is no sickness on Mars. Tiny organisms, which cause so much pain and disease on Earth, have never appeared on Mars. Or perhaps the Martians got rid of them long ago.

It seems to me that the Martians were once beings like us. Then their brains grew huge and their arms grew into tentacles. The rest of the Martian body disappeared over time. Machines took over the work of the body.

We men have our bicycles and roller skates, our machines, our guns and sticks, and so forth. But we are only at the beginning of what the Martians have become. The Martians are nothing but brains. They wear different bodies, or fighting machines, as they need them, just as we wear different clothes.

Oddly enough, with all their machinery, the Martians have not made use of the wheel. Instead, their machinery has sliding parts much like muscles and joints. That is why their machines seem so much like living animals.

I sat for hours at a time watching the sluggish Martians and their graceful machines—until the clergyman jerked on my arm and demanded a turn.

10 The Days of Imprisonment

It was dangerous to watch the Martians so closely. But the clergyman and I could not take our eyes off them. We would race up to the hole as quietly as we could, then fight for a place in front of it. We would hit and kick each other while the Martians worked a few feet away.

The fact is, the clergyman and I could not get along. Being in danger together made it worse. I had come to hate his weakness. I hated the way he would cry for hours at a time. I sometimes thought he would make me lose my mind.

The clergyman ate more than I did. I tried to tell him that we had to save as much food as possible. But he would not listen.

I hated to do it, but at last I threatened him and finally hit him. This helped for a time. But he was too weak and selfish to control himself for long.

I do not like to write these things. But I set them down so that nothing will be left out of my story. People who have escaped the dark side of life will find it easy to blame me. They know what is wrong as well as any, but they don't know what can happen to tortured men.

While we fought in whispers and grabbed food and drink, the Martians worked. The day came when the Martians brought men into the pit. The clergyman was watching when it happened. He did not say a word, but he suddenly moved back from the hole in the wall in a panic. I took his place and looked out.

Before me was a Martian in a fighting machine. I saw a long tentacle reaching over the shoulder of the machine to a little cage on its back. Then something was lifted high into the sky.

It was a man. He was heavy, middle-aged, and well dressed. Three days ago he had been an important fellow. I could see his staring eyes and his gold cuff links and watch chains shining in the light. The Martians carried him out of sight. For a moment there was silence. Then came screaming and a happy hooting sound from the Martians.

I clapped my hands over my ears and ran into the basement. I did not look out the hole again for most of the day. Then I thought I would dig a tunnel and escape. With a hatchet, I began digging as quietly as I could. But when the hole was only a few feet deep, the earth caved in, making a noise as it fell. I did not dare try again.

A few days later, I sat at the peephole for some time. Suddenly, I knew I was alone. I went quietly back to the kitchen. There was the clergyman, drinking. I reached out in the dark and grabbed a bottle of wine.

For a few minutes, we fought. The bottle broke. We stood, out of breath, making threats. Finally, I put myself between him and the food. I divided the food into small piles; there was enough for ten more days. I would not let him eat any more that day. He cried and said over and over how hungry he was. I was tired, but I did not give in.

For two days we fought in whispers and quiet kicks and blows. Sometimes I beat him and kicked him madly. At other times I tried to reason with him. Nothing worked. He kept trying to get at the food.

Then he began talking to himself out loud, putting us both in danger. Slowly, I began to see that his mind had gone. One day, he began to talk loudly. I could do nothing to quiet him.

"Be still!" I begged him.

"I have been still too long," he said loudly. "And now I must speak my mind! Woe to the Earth! Woe! Woe! Woe!"

"Shut up!" I said. I was terribly afraid that the Martians would hear us.

"No!" said the clergyman, at the top of his voice. He held out his arms. "Speak! The word of the Lord is upon me!" In three steps he was at the kitchen door.

"I go!" he said. "I have waited too long!"

I put out my hand and felt the meat chopper hanging on the wall. In a flash I was after him. I was crazed with fear. Before he was halfway across the kitchen, I was upon him.

With one last touch of kindness, I turned back the blade and hit him with the butt. He fell to the floor. I stood over him, panting. He lay still.

Suddenly I heard a noise from outside. Some plaster slipped and fell. The opening of the hole went dark. I saw the lower part of a Martian machine moving across the hole. Then one of its metal tentacles reached slowly through the hole.

I turned and almost fell over the clergyman. I stopped at the door to the basement. The tentacle was now in the kitchen. It twisted and turned with strange sudden movements, this way and that.

For a while I stood and stared. Then, with a low cry, I forced myself out of the kitchen. I ran to the coal cellar and stood there listening.

Something was moving back and forth in the kitchen. Then a heavy body—I knew too well what— was dragged across the floor of the kitchen. I had to look. I went quietly to the kitchen door and peeped in. The tentacle was touching the clergyman's head.

I stole quietly back to the coal cellar and shut the door. As best I could, I covered myself with wood and coal.

Soon I heard the tentacle moving about again. I thought it might be too short to reach me. I waited. Then I heard it turn the doorknob. It had found the door. The Martians understood doors!

In a minute, the door was open. I could just see the thing in the darkness. It was more like an elephant's trunk than anything else. It was waving toward me. It touched the wood, the coal, the ceiling.

Once, even, it touched the heel of my boot. I thought I would scream. I bit my hand.

For a time, it was still. Then the tentacle closed the cellar door. I heard it reach into the pantry. Cans rattled and a bottle smashed. There was a heavy bump against the cellar door and then silence.

"Had it gone?" I wondered.

At last I decided that it had. It did not come past the kitchen again. But I lay in the darkness of the coal cellar all that day and the next.

I did not dare go into the kitchen for several days. When I finally looked out the hole once more, the Martians had gone. The pit was empty except for the skeletons of the dead. The red weed was growing everywhere.

I was free at last. I had been inside the house for 15 long days.

11 The Man on Putney Hill

After being inside for so long, the day seemed wonderfully bright. The sky glowed blue. The red weed moved gently in the breeze. And oh! The sweetness of the air!

For a long time, I stood and looked around me. I expected to see wrecked houses. Instead, the place had the look of another planet. The red weed covered almost everything.

I felt that this place belonged to humankind no more but to the Martians. I was no longer a master but one of the animals under the Martian heel. Like animals, we would watch and run and hide.

I made my way toward Kew. Everywhere I looked, the red weed was growing. In the end, it died as quickly as it had spread. It was killed by some earthly disease. At the time, however, it grew full and thick and blood red.

On top of Putney Hill, I found an inn and some food. I settled down to spend the night.

I thought about the clergyman. I was not sorry for what I had done. But the memory did not set well with me. I was agitated about that moment of anger and fear.

I thought back to the day we had first met, when he paid no attention to my thirst. We had never been able to get along. If I had guessed what would happen, I would have left him at Halliford. But I did not guess, and that is no crime.

No one else saw the death of the clergyman. I might have kept it a secret. But I write it down, as I have written down everything else that happened. The reader must decide if I am guilty or not.

When I was done thinking about the dead clergyman, I wondered about my wife. Suddenly, the night became terrible. I could imagine a hundred things. I found myself praying that the heat ray had killed her quickly and without causing pain.

At dawn I left the inn. I thought of going to Leatherhead. I knew, however, that I had only the smallest chance of finding my wife there. Perhaps, though, I could learn where she had escaped.

As I came near Wimbledon Common, I had the feeling of being watched. A man rose up from a row of bushes, holding a sword. I walked up to him slowly. He stood silently, not moving.

His clothes were as dusty as my own. Black hair fell over his eyes. There was a red cut across his face. At first, I did not know him.

"It is you," he said. "Weren't you killed at Weybridge?"

"You are the artilleryman!" I said.

"Good luck!" he said. "We are the lucky ones!" He put out a hand, and I took it.

"Have you seen any Martians?" I asked.

"They've gone away to London," he said. "They've got a bigger camp there. At night the sky is alive with their lights. From here, you can just see them moving about in their fighting machines."

He continued, "I saw a couple of them near Hammersmith carrying something big. And the night before last, there was something up in the air. I believe they're learning to build flying machines."

"Flying machines!" I said. "If they can do that, it's all over for us. They will go around the world."

He nodded. "It's over," he said. "It isn't a war. It never was a war. It's as if they were men and we were ants. Only . . ."

"We're edible ants," I said.

We sat looking at each other. "And what will they do with us?" I said.

"Right now, they catch us when they need us," he said. "But they won't keep on doing that. First they'll smash our guns and ships and trains. Then they'll pick up the best of us and keep us in cages and things. Lord! They haven't begun on us yet!"

"Not begun!" I said.

"Not begun," he said. "They don't want to bother with us yet. They're busy making the things they need. But it's no good trying to blow them up or anything. Instead, we've got to get ready for the new state of things."

After a few minutes, I asked, "What shall we do?"

"It's like this. We have to make a new sort of life, safe enough to live in and bring up children. But we must not become savagelike . . . You see, I intend to live underground. Under London are miles and miles of drains. With London empty, after a few days' rain they'll be clean. And they're big and airy enough for everyone. Eh? Do you begin to see?"

He went on. "What we'll do is get strong, clean-minded men. Clean-minded women, too—mothers and teachers. Anyone else would spoil the race. But we must do more than save the race. We can't just live like rats.

"That's where men like you come in," he continued. "We must make safe places down deep. We must get all the books we can. Not novels and poetry, but scientific books. We must keep up our science, learn more. We must watch the Martians. Some of us must be spies. When it's all working, maybe I'll be a spy."

The artilleryman laid a brown hand on my arm. "Just think of this," he said. "Just think of four or five of their fighting machines taking off—driven by men! Just think of the Martians when they see fighting machines taking off without them!

"They'll come puffing and blowing up to their

other machines. But those machines won't work. There will be something out of gear in every one. And just as they're fussing over a machine, swish comes the heat ray! And the world will be ours again."

For a while, I believed all he said. Then we went to the house where he had been working.

The artilleryman was digging a tunnel from the coal cellar to the main drain on Putney Hill. So far, it was about ten yards long. It had taken him a week to do a day's work. I began to see the gap between his dreams and his powers.

Still, I believed in him enough to begin digging. We worked all that morning until past noon.

"We're working quite well," he said. "Let's knock off a bit."

"But the work?" I said.

"Oh, one can't always work," he said. "We ought to take a look around for Martians now."

We went to the roof of the house. He began talking of his grand plans again. He made them sound wonderful. I half believed in him once more.

We came down from the roof, but neither of us felt like working. He suggested a meal, and I agreed. Then he brought out some fine cigars.

"There's champagne in the cellar," he said.

"We can dig better on wine," I said.

"No," he said. "You are my guest tonight.

Champagne! We have enough work before us! Let us take a rest while we may."

We drank, and he insisted that we play cards. We gambled for pieces of land around London. And it is strange to say so, but it was delightful! How odd is the mind of man. There was nothing before us but death. Yet we could enjoy playing cards!

We spent a long time playing cards. Then we ate again. The artilleryman finished the champagne, and we smoked. After a while, I took a cigar and went upstairs alone.

I looked out across the valley and thought about my dear wife. Suddenly, I was sick at myself. I threw down my cigar in disgust. I decided then to leave the artilleryman to his dreaming and drinking and eating. I would go to London and learn what men and the Martians were doing.

12 Wreckage

After I had left the artilleryman, I went down the hill, across the bridge to Fulham, and on to London. The red weed almost covered the bridge. But it was beginning to turn white with disease. Its red color was fading; its branches were drying and breaking off. Black dust covered the road from the bridge onward. It grew thicker as I went. Where there was no black dust, it seemed like any quiet Sunday in London.

The streets were empty and terribly quiet. Then I heard a noise in the distance. It was a sobbing, howling sound: ulla, ulla, ulla, ulla. It kept on without stopping.

I walked on, tired, hungry, and terribly lonely. I wondered why I was walking in this city of the dead. I thought of the poisons in the pharmacies.

I broke into a restaurant and got food and drink. I slept on a sofa behind the bar for a while. When I woke up, the howling was still going on: ulla, ulla, ulla, ulla. I ate some biscuits, then went out again.

As I came to the top of Baker Street, I could see a fighting machine in the distance. I was not frightened. Perhaps I was too tired to be afraid. The machine did not move but simply stood still, as the Martian inside howled.

I pushed on toward Primrose Hill. As I crossed a bridge, the howling suddenly stopped. The silence came like a clap of thunder.

On the curve of Primrose Hill, I saw another fighting machine. It stood perfectly still, like the first. A crazy idea came over me. I could die and end it all for myself. I would not even have the trouble of killing myself.

I marched on toward the fighting machine. Then I saw a number of black birds about its hood. At that, my heart jumped. I began to run up the hill toward the machine.

I reached the top and looked down. Below me was a big pit the Martians had dug. Here and there were huge machines. And all around lay Martians—dead!

They, like the red weed, had been killed by disease. After all human efforts had failed, the Martians, nonetheless, now lay dead. They had been killed by the smallest things that God, in his wisdom, had put upon Earth—tiny organisms.

At the time, I did not know how they had died. But as I stared into the pit, my heart lit up inside me. On the far lip of the hole, huge and strange, lay the great flying machine we so feared. Death had come not a day too soon!

I looked out over London. This great, dead city

would once more come to life. These black, burned streets would soon ring with the noise of hammers. I reached my hands toward the sky and began to thank God. In a year, I thought. In a year . . .

Then I thought of my wife. Our old life of hope and tenderness was gone forever!

Of the next three days, I knew nothing. I have learned since that others, too, discovered the dead Martians. One man wired the news to Paris. From there, it was flashed all over the world.

Already men cried with joy, shook hands, and shouted. They filled the trains back to London. Church bells rang up and down England. Countries everywhere sent food. All the ships in the world seemed headed for London then. But I cannot remember any of this.

Some people found me in St. John's Wood. I had been crying and saying, "The last man left alive! Hurrah! The last man left alive!"

They were very kind people who found me. They took me in. When my mind was clear again, they gently told me the news. Leatherhead had been destroyed. Everyone in the town had been killed.

I was a sad and lonely man, and the people were good to me. I stayed with them four days. But soon I wanted to see what was left of my little life.

It was a bright day when I went back to Maybury Hill. The streets were very busy. At Waterloo, free

trains were taking people to their homes.

The station near Maybury Hill was being repaired. So I walked from Byfleet. When I saw our house, I had a quick flash of hope. But it was empty. My muddy footprints from the night of the storm were still there. My work was still on my desk.

I came downstairs to the dining room. There was the bread and meat, now rotten, that I had shared with the artilleryman.

Then I heard a voice say, "This house is empty. No one has been here for ten days. No one has escaped but you."

I jumped. Had I spoken aloud? I walked up to the French window and looked out.

Standing there were my cousin and my wife. My wife cried quietly.

"I came," she said. "I knew . . . I knew . . ."

She put her hand to her throat and began to fall. I stepped forward and caught her in my arms.

Epilogue

There is still much that we do not know about the Martians. We don't know what their black smoke was made of. We don't know how their heat rays worked. A more serious question is whether the Martians will ever attack again. I think we should be more prepared in case that happens.

One man, Lessing, believes that the Martians may have landed on Venus. Seven months ago, Mars and Venus were in line with the sun. At that time, wavy markings appeared on both planets.

Whether or not the Martians come again, our thinking has changed. We no longer see Earth as a perfectly safe place. Our eyes are on other planets now. Perhaps we, too, shall be looking for a new home someday, as the Martians did. For our planet, too, is cooling.

Sometimes I have a great dream. I think of life spreading slowly from our planet far out into space. But that is a dream. Perhaps the Martians will attack once more and truly beat us the next time. Perhaps the future belongs to them.

I know those days of danger have filled my mind with dark thoughts. Sometimes as I sit at night writing, I suddenly see the valley below consumed in flames. My dreams are ugly and frightening.

How strange it is to stand once more on Primrose Hill, as I did some days ago. How strange to see families walking about and looking at the Martian machine that still stands there today. Strangest of all is to hold my dear wife's hand again and to think that I once counted her among the dead, as she counted me!